MW01442387

A Catholic Confession of Faith

We Pray

Growing Spiritually through the
Catechism of the Catholic Church

Part Four: Prayer

Deacon Henry Libersat

Pauline
BOOKS & MEDIA
Boston

Imprimatur:
† Norbert M. Dorsey, C.P.
Bishop of Orlando
January 22, 1997

Library of Congress Cataloging-in-Publication Data

Libersat, Henry.
  We pray : growing spiritually through the Catechism of the
Catholic Church / Henry Libersat.
     p.   cm. — (A Catholic confession of faith)
   ISBN 0-8198-8291-7 (pbk.)
   1. Prayer—Catholic Church. 2. Lord's prayer. 3. Catholic
Church. Catechismus Ecclesiae Catholicæ. 4. Catholic Church—
Catechisms. I. Title. II. Series: Libersat, Henry. Catholic
confession of faith.
BV215.L53   1997
248.3'2—dc21   96-37932
                                                   CIP

The Scripture quotations contained herein are from the *New Revised
Standard Version Bible: Catholic Edition,* copyright © 1996 and 1989
by the Division of Christian Education of the National Council of
Churches of Christ in the U.S.A. Used by permission. All rights
reserved.

English translation of the *Catechism of the Catholic Church* for the
United States of America copyright © 1994, United States Catholic
Conference, Inc.—Libreria Editrice Vaticana. Used with permission.

Copyright © 1997, Henry Libersat

Printed and published in the U.S.A. by Pauline Books & Media, 50
St. Paul's Avenue, Boston, MA 02130.

http://www.pauline.org

E-mail: PBM_EDIT@INTERRAMP.COM

Pauline Books & Media is the publishing house of the Daughters of
St. Paul, an international congregation of women religious serving
the Church with the communications media.

1 2 3 4   99 98 97

Thanks and Dedication

In a small country cemetery between Henry, Louisiana and Erath, Louisiana, lie the remains of my father and mother, Henry (Sr.) and Elda Libersat. Nearby lie Pierre and Olive, my paternal grandparents. Other relatives are buried there and in another country cemetery in Bancker, Louisiana. Still others lie in Texas and Florida, for example, my maternal grandparents, Clay and Cora Zeringue.

These relatives have been a great part of my life, even since their death. They all loved me and cared for me in so many different ways. They were all Catholic and lived the faith as best they could, given their understanding of it. They all knew and loved God.

I want to dedicate *A Catholic Confession of Faith,* to them all. This "work" is actually four small books, *We Believe, We Celebrate the Mystery, We Live the Good Life,* and *We Pray.*

But in a very special way, these four books are dedicated to the memory of my wonderful parents, whose love for God and the Church gave me the foundation for my life as husband, father and grandfather, as well as for my recent decade of ministry in the Catholic Church as a deacon and for my nearly four decades of service in the Catholic press.

Thanks, Mom. Thanks, Dad.

Thanks, too, to those many priests, sisters and faithful laity whose example, love and encouragement have kept me trying to live the good life.

Truly, I am grateful to the bishop-publishers of *The Florida Catholic* for the opportunity to serve God and the Church through that interdiocesan publishing venture. I am grateful for their trust and pastoral guidance.

I am also grateful to the Daughters of St. Paul for their confidence in me and for their encouragement in my extra-curricular writing. This series brings to six the number of books I have written for Pauline Books & Media. The first two, *Way, Truth and Life* and *Do Whatever He Tells You* are presentations of our Catholic faith from a perspective of daily life. They are rooted in doctrine, Scripture and prayer, but are written in a more popular style. While I have tried to use real-life stories in this series, the books here are a bit more formal in presentation and more directly concerned with Church teaching as presented in the *Catechism of the Catholic Church*.

Given the reader response to the material as it was presented in *The Florida Catholic,* I have high hopes that these books will help many other readers. In series form in the newspaper, the material was used by many people in religious education, Re-Membering Church and RCIA, as well as for personal reflection.

Contents

CHAPTER 1
What Is Prayer ? How Do We Pray?.................................. 15

CHAPTER 2
Prayer Begins with God's Call 19

CHAPTER 3
Prayer in Salvation History.. 23

CHAPTER 4
Prayer: A Wellspring of Life 29

CHAPTER 5
Prayer: The Agonies and the Ecstasies 33

CHAPTER 6
The Battle of Prayer... 37

CHAPTER 7
The Prayer of Jesus 41

CHAPTER 8
The Lord's Prayer Revisited 45

CHAPTER 9
We Dare to Say, "Our Father" 49

CHAPTER 10
The Seven Petitions of the Lord's Prayer 53

About *A Catholic Confession of Faith...*

I thought I was "riding high" when Pauline Books & Media agreed to print a revision of two series of articles in book form. *We Believe* and *We Celebrate the Mystery* had already been published in *The Florida Catholic*. I had done what I started out to do. Honestly, I thought I was "written out" for at least another few months.

When Sister Mary Mark of Pauline Books & Media mentioned yet two more books, one on morality and one on prayer, I inwardly gulped but immediately said, "Yes, I will be happy to do them!" I gulped because I realized the amount of work I was taking on. But I immediately agreed to do the two other books for three good reasons.

First, it was a good idea and one I would share first of all with readers of *The Florida Catholic*. This statewide Catholic newspaper is my first professional love. Second, it seemed the Holy Spirit was talking to the Sisters: *We Believe* shared the content of our faith; *We Celebrate the Mystery* spoke of the awesome and loving presence of God in our sacramental life. Now, *We Live the Good Life* will help people refocus on how we respond to God's great love, and *We Pray* will discuss the wonderful ways God invites us into a personal relationship with him. Third, I realized I must personally revisit my own response to God's love, and the *Catechism of the Catholic Church* would be a wonderful aid in this task. Doing the books would make me do what I needed to do.

Each chapter in these four books ends with a reflection which will hopefully help individuals and groups to think about and discuss the material presented.

It is my prayer that all readers will benefit in reading *A Catholic Confession of Faith* as I did in writing them. The work was a joy; the response to the work was a blessing. May it give glory to God who is Father, Son and Spirit!

Deacon Henry Libersat
Pentecost, 1996

We Pray...
About This Book...

In my ministry as a deacon of the Church, I often hear people speak of the difficulty they have in praying. Growth in the knowledge and love of God requires prayer. Without prayer, we cannot begin to claim to be Christian. At the same time, I think most people pray much more than they realize.

As I mention in these pages, one of the most comforting lines in Scripture is from Romans: "Likewise the Spirit helps us in our weakness; for we do not know how to pray as we ought, but that very Spirit intercedes with sighs too deep for words" (Rom 8:26). God loves us so much that he puts our needs into prayer for us. Also, I think the anguish parents feel over wayward children and their sometimes helpless plea, "Oh, dear God! Help!" is true prayer.

But Christians cannot and should not be satisfied with prayer-by-accident or prayer that occurs only when one needs something. As we know, prayer comprises praise, thanksgiving, petition and contrition. We must praise God, thank God for all our blessings, ask God for what we truly need (and the wisdom to discern the difference between need and whim), and tell God we are sorry when we have sinned.

We Pray is the final of four books in the series *A Catholic Confession of Faith.* It takes its inspiration and direction from the *Catechism of the Catholic Church.* I am deeply grateful to Bishop Norbert M. Dorsey, CP, trustee of the partnership of bishop-publishers of *The Florida Catholic,* for permission to redo this material which first appeared in that statewide newspaper. Bishop Thomas J. Grady was my consultant and adviser for the work in these pages. For his patience and guidance I give thanks to him and to God. My wife, Peg, is my dearest and most constant friend without whom I would be so terribly impoverished! Thanks!

I hope and pray that these pages will help readers understand better the nature and purpose of prayer, the need to pray and even how to pray. I am convinced that one of the most important parts of this book is the reflection on the Lord's Prayer. When that section was published in *The Florida Catholic,* it elicited much favorable response from readers. I hope you, too, are satisfied and edified and that God will be glorified by this book and the other three in the series.

Deacon Henry Libersat
Advent, 1996

CHAPTER 1

What Is Prayer? How Do We Pray?

She died in 1984, but my memory of her goes way back. One special remembrance keeps returning. One day when I was four years old, Mama sat in her rocking chair in the living room while I was seated at her feet on the floor. Very slowly, Mama was reciting the Our Father and the Hail Mary and waiting for me to repeat each line. That's how I learned to pray. That's how I learned the name of Jesus, at my Mama's feet.

Now that I'm older, I remember other things about Mama and prayer. I remember how positively she faced whatever came our way—good times as well as bad. She had a certain serenity, a peace of heart. She could be deeply wounded by loved ones or experience searing physical pain, yet still she was at peace. Her peace was rooted in faith, but a faith that expressed itself in surrender, not just in a nod of assent to doctrine or creed or God's will. Although she never would have dreamed or dared to claim such, her peace was rooted in her deep personal relationship with God.

She didn't think she was good enough for God; she knew her shortcomings. But she had faith in God, trusted God, loved God—and she loved us all no matter what happened or how much we disappointed her. Mama's greatest prayer was her life. She lived it to the full and she lived it for us and for God.

Most of us can remember our parents or grandparents teaching us to "say our prayers," which was good training. The formal prayers of the Church help us think about and vocalize the important parts of our relationship with God: our dependence on God and our need to worship, love and serve him, as well as our need for his mercy.

The Lord's Prayer is the *perfect* prayer because it came from the lips, mind and heart of Jesus. In that prayer, we first of all worship God: he is Father, in heaven; his name is holy; his kingdom must come and his will must be done.

Second, we acknowledge our dependence on God and our need for his kindness, mercy and support. We need him to give us our daily bread—and that means whatever we need, since all comes from God, even our hard-earned paycheck. We need his forgiveness and we need to forgive others; we need him to protect us in times of temptation and to deliver us from all evil. In this second half of the Lord's Prayer, which we call the Our Father, we give our entire lives to God—the past, the present and the future. We pray for what we need today (present); we ask forgiveness and forgive offenses (past); we ask God to protect us from temptation and deliver us from evil (future). This perfect prayer puts God first and praises him, acknowledges our dependence on him and gives him our entire lives—past, present and future.

The *Catechism of the Catholic Church* reminds us that St. Therese of Lisieux called prayer a "surge of the heart" (no. 2558). She said it was turning one's eyes to heaven in "a cry of recognition and of love" which embraces "both trial and joy."

During a retreat many years ago, someone asked a well-known nun, Mother Angelica of the Eternal Word

What Is Prayer? How Do We Pray?　　17

Television Network, "What is the best way to pray?" She replied, "The best way to pray is the way you pray best." That answer contains wisdom. It puts people at ease with the notion of praying; it is also open ended, allowing people to grow in depth and breadth of prayer.

Catholics pray in many different ways: silent and contemplative prayer, novenas, the rosary, praying the Scriptures, reciting favorite prayers. Of course, the Mass is the greatest of prayers and our highest form of prayer. The *Catechism* calls us to a deep understanding of prayer. It is not enough merely to "say prayers." Actually, "saying prayers" can sometimes fall short of really praying. Here are some of the things we learn about prayer from the *Catechism* (cf. nos. 2562-2565):

> Prayer involves the whole person. It is the "whole man who prays." However, Scripture sometimes speaks of the soul or the heart of a person as the source of prayer. It is "the *heart* that prays. If our heart is far from God, the words of prayer are in vain."

> The heart is the dwelling-place where I am, where I live.... The heart is our hidden center, beyond the grasp of our reason and of others; only the Spirit of God can fathom the human heart and know it fully. The heart is the place of decision, deeper than our psychic drives. It is the place of truth, where we choose life or death. It is the place of encounter, because as image of God we live in relation: it is the place of covenant.

> Christian prayer is a covenant relationship between God and man in Christ. It is the action of God and of man, springing forth from both the Holy Spirit and ourselves, wholly directed to the Father, in union with the human will of the Son of God made man.

In the New Covenant, prayer is the living relationship of the children of God with their Father who is good beyond measure, with his Son Jesus Christ and with the Holy Spirit.... The life of prayer is the habit of being in the presence of the thrice-holy God and in communion with him. This communion of life is always possible because, through Baptism, we have already been united with Christ. Prayer is *Christian* insofar as it is communion with Christ and extends throughout the Church, which is his Body. Its dimensions are those of Christ's love.

Perhaps the prophet Micah (6:8) sums it up very well, without even mentioning "prayer": "He has told you, O mortal, what is good; and what does the Lord require of you but to do justice, and to love kindness, and to walk humbly with your God?"

Reflection:

- How can prayer become a good habit?
- Discuss with a friend how you pray best. Do you use formal prayer? Do you prefer simply to talk to God? Do you listen to God?

CHAPTER **2**

Prayer Begins with God's Call

O Lord, our Sovereign,
how majestic is your name in all the earth!
You have set your glory above the heavens.
Out of the mouths of babes and infants
you have founded a bulwark because of your foes,
to silence the enemy and the avenger.
When I look at your heavens,
the work of your fingers,
the moon and the stars that you have established;
what are human beings that you are mindful of them,
mortals that you care for them?
Yet you have made them a little lower than God,
and crowned them with glory and honor.
You have given them dominion over the works of
    your hands;
you have put all things under their feet,
all sheep and oxen,
and also the beasts of the field,
the birds of the air, and the fish of the sea,
whatever passes along the paths of the seas.
O Lord, our Sovereign,
how majestic is your name in all the earth!

Psalm 8

People sometimes say something to the effect, "When I read the psalms, something happens inside. I feel good. I feel so close to God that somehow it seems I can pray better."

No wonder! The psalms are prayers of praise, petition and contrition. Psalm 8, cited above, is one of great praise. The person beginning a search for God, as well as the confirmed believer, finds here a wonderful prayer of praise. The soul stands in wonder before its Creator. The more confirmed a believer, the more one prays, and the more meaning one finds in the psalm.

The same is true for the formal prayers of the Church: the Our Father, Hail Mary, Glory Be, the Creed and all acts of contrition, hope, faith and love. The closer one comes to God, the more one prays, the more one hungers for God, and the more one *wants to pray*. Prayer is at this point no longer a chore, but a thrill, a joy, a most perfect expression and experience of freedom.

Of course, even the greatest of saints at times didn't feel like praying and didn't seem to "get anything out of prayer." Prayer is not only something we get; it is also something we give. We give glory to God and praise and worship him. Even when we don't feel like praying, have serious distractions, or would rather be on a picnic or out water skiing, if we persist in prayer, surrendering our will to God's, then we are indeed praying. At such times, our prayer may be a greater act of faith and worship than at times when we are emotionally disposed to pray and "feel good" about praying.

The *Catechism of the Catholic Church* reminds us: "Man is in search of God" (no. 2566). Even the effects of sin cannot touch the deep inner longing each human being has for God. Sometimes people search for God in ways which are far from God, but their quest for happiness is genuine. However misguided one's ways of seeking happiness may be, a longing for God throbs at the core and heart of every human being. St. Augustine said it well: "You have made us for yourself, O Lord, and our heart is restless until it rests in you."

The *Catechism* puts it this way: "God calls man first.... The living and true God tirelessly calls each person to that mysterious encounter known as prayer. In prayer, the faithful God's initiative of love always comes first; our own first step is always a response" (no. 2567). In other words, we do not initiate prayer; we only respond to God's call to us. We could not respond to God unless the call echoed in each human heart to return to our Source and our End, the Lord God.

God called us into life by creating us from nothing. He gave us a paradise in which to live. He walked in the cool of the evening with us, yet we sinned. As the *Catechism* points out, again God called out to us: "Where are you?... What is this that you have done?" (Gen 3:9, 13). And then, finally, the cry of the new Adam, Jesus the Christ: "I have come to do your will, O God" (Heb 10:7).

In the Letter to the Romans, we learn just how much God longs for us to be with him: "The Spirit helps us in our weakness; for we do not know how to pray as we ought, but that very Spirit intercedes with sighs too deep for words. And God, who searches the heart, knows what is the mind of the Spirit, because the Spirit intercedes for the saints according to the will of God" (Rom 8:26-27).

Reflection:

- Have you ever found it hard to pray? Why? Distractions? Fatigue? Boredom? Doubt? What have you learned from that experience?

- Read prayerfully and carefully Psalm 8 above.

CHAPTER 3

Prayer in Salvation History

Easter
By Thomas J. Grady

The high speed *Zephyr*
glides out of Union Station in Chicago,
smoothly building up power.
Out of the window, people blur.
Even towns melt together
as they flash by.
In less than three hours
the *Zephyr* eases into Dubuque, Iowa.
At 9 p.m. the *Zephyr* leaves Dubuque.
In the dark of the night only the speeding stars
seem motionless and unblinking.
Below, houses gleam like sparks of light.
Towns huddle together into one glow of light.
Midnight, the *Zephyr* glides
into Union Station, Chicago
where it began.
Life is like that,
swiftly gathering momentum,
flashing by.
Going and coming,
and being back

WE PRAY

at where it all started.
Off to school and back from school;
off to work and back from work;
off to the brightness of marriage
and back, when the flowers fade,
to the sameness of married life,
back and forth going nowhere.
The French have words for it.
Ennui, weariness, boredom.
Camus labels us each *stranger,*
stranger: strangers to each other,
strangers to the world,
riding the swift, indifferent train to nowhere.
But HE says, "Stop!"
Feel the slowness and warmth of *love.*
Love, making persons out of blurs,
making formless towns
into sharing communities.
Love, making the destination
the trip.
Life hereafter being lived now.
"As the Father has loved me,
I have loved you.
love one another
as I have loved you.
Live on in my love."
Weariness is shared
with the tired man at Jacob's well.
All life's pain
is shared with someone
who opened his arms to us
on a cross.
The emptiness of life
is transformed

by the emptiness of the tomb.
The dreariness of life
is transformed to joy
by the glory
of the one who rose
from the dead for us,
and who is with us
and waits for us.

This beautiful poem, a prayerful reflection, a prayer in itself, was written by the Most Reverend Thomas J. Grady, retired bishop of the Orlando Diocese. It was first published in the 1996 Lenten reflections in the statewide newspaper, *The Florida Catholic.*

Bishop Grady's poem serves well to demonstrate what the *Catechism of the Catholic Church* teaches: "Prayer is lived in the first place beginning with the realities of *creation*" (no. 2569).

One key word here is that prayer is "lived," not recited nor memorized. It is lived! Yes, we do speak memorized prayers—but we have to will to pray if we are to pray. Otherwise, we may be involved only in saying words out of habit. True, we are distracted. Distractions do not negate our intention to pray as long as we make an effort to set them aside or, as one priest advised years ago, to bring those distractions consciously into prayer and see why they are so distracting.

Why does the beauty of creation inspire us to pray? An experience shared by two men may help:

Stretched out under the stars on the bleachers of a football stadium, the younger man, just out of high school, said to the older man, "When I look up at the stars, I feel so small, and yet, I somehow feel part of it all."

The older man, a principal of a high school, was silent for a while. Finally he said, "That's why I like to lie out here on the bleachers at night, looking up at the stars. It puts me in touch with who I am. How can I look at the vastness of space, the order of the cosmos, the beauty of the moon and stars and not think of God? This, to me, is like prayer."

"Yeah," said the younger man. "Me, too."

Something inside us, since we are part of creation, helps us see into the mystery and majesty that is beyond creation, God himself. Even before the time of Abraham, whom God called to a covenant (the ultimate communion in prayer), we know that Enoch "walked with God" and that Noah was found pleasing to God "because his heart was upright and undivided" (no. 2569).

But with Abraham salvation history took form and communication, so that covenant and communion with God became possible for humanity. We see in Abraham a man of silence whose faith was *lived* as he followed God's call. In Genesis, his prayer life takes form only in chapter 15, where he complains to God, reminding him of his promises. Before these spoken words, Abraham, our father in faith, lived his prayer by obeying the call of God and erecting altars to the one God at every stopping place (cf. no. 2570).

Because of his fidelity and willingness to hear and obey God, Abraham was properly disposed to receive God's blessings, even if they challenged logic: his aged wife would bear a son; Abraham's descendants would be more numerous than the stars or the grains of sand on the seashore. Finally, he was asked to sacrifice his only son, who was to be the means of his achieving many descendants. Faithfully, Abraham followed God's instructions, realizing that even through this seemingly impossible situ-

Prayer in Salvation History

ation God's will would be accomplished and his promises honored. We know the rest of the story. God did not let Abraham kill Isaac but provided another sacrifice instead. Abraham's faith had passed a severe test.

Later, Moses would lead the people of God and would save the Israelites from Egypt through the mighty works of God. Moses would become the great prophet, a leader who spoke with God, who saw God and yet lived. He would receive the Ten Commandments, God's concrete revelation of the natural law written in the hearts of all human beings from Adam and Eve to the most recent newborn baby. Moses was the great mediator for his people. He stood before God speaking for his people; he stood before his people speaking for God. He is the "the most striking example of intercessory prayer, which will be fulfilled in 'the one mediator between God and men, the man Christ Jesus'" (no. 2574).

Moses gained strength for his work of intercession from his intimate relationship with God. His faith gave him a great determination to fulfill God's will and to teach what God taught (no. 2577). His most striking prayer of intercession came after the people and Aaron, his brother and co-worker, had fallen victim to idolatry. Moses pleaded with God for the people, reminded God of his divine promises, and appealed to God's sense of justice.

The *Catechism* reminds us that the human experience with prayer continues through King David and the prophet Elijah (cf. nos. 2578-2584). The *Catechism* reminds us that David was the king "after God's own heart," a shepherd who became a warrior king who interceded between God and the people. David sinned grievously yet had the faith and humility to ultimately repent. His psalms grace Christian prayer to this day.

Elijah also learned of God's power and fidelity

through sacrifice and rejection. His faith grew sufficiently to influence the widow to use the last of her food for the prophet, and God rewarded her with more food, enough to last through the famine. Elijah challenged the pagan priests serving Jezebel to a "prayer duel." It was not the pagans' gods, but only the one true God, the God of Israel who, responding to the prophet's faith-filled prayer, sent fire upon the water-soaked wood to consume Elijah's sacrifice.

This victorious Elijah slew the 600 pagan priests and then fled Jezebel's men who wanted to kill him. Elijah met God in a "small whispering sound" outside the cave in which he had sought refuge (cf. 1 Kgs 19:1-14).

Concerning the psalms, the *Catechism* says they are "the masterwork of prayer in the Old Testament. They present two inseparable qualities: the personal, and the communal. They extend to all dimensions of history, recalling God's promises already fulfilled and looking for the coming of the Messiah.... Prayed and fulfilled in Christ, the Psalms are an essential and permanent element of the prayer of the Church. They are suitable for men of every condition and time" (nos. 2596-2597).

Look at creation with new eyes. "Stop! Feel the slowness and warmth of love"—the love of the one who loves as the Father loves.

Reflection:

- Have you ever "worked" at prayer? Why? What were the results?

- Has obedience ever been a prayer in your life?

- Share Bishop Grady's poem with a friend.

CHAPTER 4

Prayer: A Wellspring of Life

The elderly man sat in the back of the room, looking around in wonder. He had never seen such a sight. "This is supposed to be a Catholic parish," he thought. "Yet, all these people are singing, clapping hands and even dancing around."

After the prayer meeting, a smiling woman approached him. "Wasn't that just wonderful!" she exclaimed. "I could feel the Lord's presence with us this evening." The man simply smiled and said, "That's nice."

Since Vatican Council II, changes have affected not only the liturgy but other ways of praying. Individual and groups of Catholics have found new ways of expressing their faith in prayer. The charismatic renewal, too often misunderstood and misjudged, has been one of the most remarkable spiritual renewals to come our way in many years. Through this spiritual renewal and the experience of "baptism in the Holy Spirit," thousands of Catholics have discovered a new depth in their relationship with God, a new excitement about their Catholic faith, more reverence for the Sacred Scriptures and greater courage and energy in sharing their faith with others. We have seen tremendous results from Marriage Encounter, Retrouvaille, Cursillo and other movements as well.

They have in common a call to deeper conversion through prayer and communion with God and one another. The Holy Spirit has done all he can to help Catholics embrace the authentic renewal called for by Vatican Council II: a spiritual renewal rooted in prayer, bearing fruit in evangelization, catechesis, works of mercy and the renewal of secular society.

So, we turn to prayer. The *Catechism of the Catholic Church* reminds us that prayer "cannot be reduced to the spontaneous outpouring of interior impulse: in order to pray, one must have the will to pray" (no. 2650). The woman in our story may well have been ecstatic in prayer, but she may have been having a great time by getting emotionally involved. The deciding factor would be whether she had chosen to pray. The man in our story was taken aback by the exuberance and outward expression of love of God and prayer. He preferred a more sedate spirituality. He knew the prayers of the Church from childhood and was a person who prayed. However, the *Catechism* warns that simply knowing prayers and "what the Scriptures reveal about prayer" is not enough: "one must also learn to pray" (no. 2650).

Several "wellsprings" lead us to the Holy Spirit. "The Holy Spirit is the *living water* 'welling up to eternal life' in the heart that prays." The Holy Spirit leads us to the source of eternal life: Christ.

The *Catechism* mentions some wellsprings where the Spirit works (cf. nos. 2652-2660):

• *The Word of God* who is Jesus the Lord. To know Jesus Christ personally and intimately is the goal of every committed Christian. The Church encourages us to learn "the surpassing value of knowing Christ Jesus" (Phil 3:8) by frequent and prayerful reading of Sacred Scripture. If the Scriptures are read prayerfully, a dialogue begins between the believer and God.

• *The liturgy of the Church.* The mystery of salvation is proclaimed and made present by Jesus Christ and the Holy Spirit. This mystery of salvation continues in the heart of those who pray. "Prayer internalizes and assimilates the liturgy during and after its celebration. Even when it is lived out in 'secret,' prayer is always prayer *of the Church;* it is a communion with the Holy Trinity."

• *The theological virtues* of faith, hope and charity involve life in the Holy Spirit. We approach and celebrate the liturgy in *faith.* Faith directs us to seek Jesus, the source and end of our lives. We celebrate the liturgy with expectant faith, knowing that God hears us and loves us, and having the certainty that Christ will come again. Through the power of the Holy Spirit we can harbor and express such *hope.* And *charity* enables us to hope without fear of disappointment. God loves us and that love has been poured into our hearts by the Holy Spirit. "Prayer, formed by the liturgical life, draws everything into the love by which we are loved in Christ and which enables us to respond to him by loving as he has loved us."

• *The present moment of every day.* The Holy Spirit comes to us at all times. Those sacred moment of the liturgy can be made part and parcel of daily life through our response to the Spirit's promptings. The Spirit makes "prayer spring up from us" if we are open to his grace. "It is right and good to pray so that the coming of the kingdom of justice and peace may influence the march of history, but it is just as important to bring the help of prayer into humble, everyday situations; all forms of prayer can be the leaven to which the Lord compares the kingdom."

Prayer, then, is for all times, occasions and intentions. It is communion with the Most Holy Trinity and with all the faithful, living and dead. Prayer is the wellspring of eternal life because it unites us to Jesus through the power of the Spirit. Prayer is life-giving and healing as we praise God and intercede for ourselves and others.

We may pray to the Father, to Jesus and to the Spirit. We may pray to and with Holy Mary and all the saints. Freely willed and embraced, prayer links us with salvation history and Christ's salvific power.

Reflection:

- How do you prefer to pray? Has anyone else made you uncomfortable with their prayer style?

- Explain the differences between knowing prayers and praying.

CHAPTER 5

Prayer: The Agonies and the Ecstasies

The sun shone through the majestic oaks as the clouds sailed by, turning the dead leaves on the ground into a patchwork of light and shadow. But the man didn't see the clouds or the light as he plodded through the grounds surrounding the chapel. Birds sang, but he did not hear. A spider wove a web, but he did not see. The breeze gently fanned the skin of his hands and face, but he did not feel.

He made his way into the chapel and knelt before the tabernacle. Shadows deepened as the clouds again hid the sun. He "saw" the darkness, which was the color of his mood, maybe even his soul, as he pondered his problems.

As he knelt before the tabernacle, he poured out his misery to God. He was lost, confused, hurting, unsure of his future. As he prayed, he began, little by little, to turn his problems over to God. A phrase echoed from his boyhood preparation for first Holy Communion: "All for thee, O Lord!" He repeated that phrase over and over again. His spirits began to lift. Outside the clouds floated away and the sun sparkled through the stained glass. A sunbeam shone on the tabernacle as the man prayed, "All for thee, O Lord!" His gloom lifted as he saw the tabernacle bathed in golden light. He felt the presence of the

33

Lord and the nearness of his love. As the man left the chapel a while later, he noticed the sunlight, the clouds, the trees and the spider.

No wonder that this man, and so many other Catholics, find solace in prayer before the Blessed Sacrament, the physical and spiritual presence of Jesus in the Sacred Host. Jesus is the way of all prayer.

The Holy Spirit teaches us how to pray. Again, we recall the marvelous truth that when we cannot pray, the Spirit prays within us and for us to the Father (cf. Rom 8:26). The Holy Spirit teaches us to pray "in the name of Jesus." No one can even say "Jesus is Lord" without the grace of the Holy Spirit (cf. 1 Cor 12:3).

The name of Jesus says it all. When we say "Jesus," we have said: Son of God, Son of Mary, Savior, Redeemer, Friend, Brother, Lord. Just prayerfully and reflectively saying the name of Jesus over and over is a marvelous prayer in itself. As the *Catechism of the Catholic Church* teaches:

> The name "Jesus" contains all: God and man and the whole economy of creation and salvation. To pray "Jesus" is to invoke him and to call him within us. His name is the only one that contains the presence it signifies. Jesus is the Risen One, and whoever invokes the name of Jesus is welcoming the Son of God who loved him and gave himself up for him (no. 2666).

During our formal prayers, especially at Mass, we pray "through Jesus Christ who lives and reigns with you and the Holy Spirit, one God for ever and ever. Amen!" Despite variations in the wording, the meaning is the same. We are praying *in the name of Jesus.*

Part of the ecstasy of prayer is intellectual—simply knowing that by praying we are responding to God's

Prayer: The Agonies and the Ecstasies

grace, to his call to be one with him in a deep and loving communion. Prayer also has an emotional ecstasy—we sometimes *feel* the presence of God. Like the man in our story, the gloom fades before the joy and glory of the knowledge that God is with us.

We pray to the Father in the name of Jesus; we pray to Jesus; we pray to the Holy Spirit, but all our prayer is through Jesus. We could not even speak God's name had he not revealed it to us: "The divine name may not be spoken by human lips, but by assuming our humanity the Word of God hands it over to us and we can invoke it: 'Jesus,' 'YHWH saves'" (no. 2666).

Our Catholic faith is deeply rooted in the presence and activity of the Holy Spirit. We pray, "Come Holy Spirit...." At Mass we ask God to send the Holy Spirit on the gifts of bread and wine so they can become the Body and Blood of Jesus the Lord.

Another joy in our Catholic prayer life is our close relationship with Mary. Through the liturgical year at Mass, and through such private devotions as the rosary, we walk with Mary through the life of her Son. Moreover, our rich tradition tells us that Mary intercedes for us as we ask her to help us in prayer to God for any of our needs. Whenever we pray, we pray in communion with the Church and in communion with Mary, and this by the power of the Holy Spirit:

> In prayer the Holy Spirit unites us to the person of the only Son, in his glorified humanity, through which and in which our filial prayer unites us in the Church with the Mother of Jesus (no. 2673).

Traditionally, Catholics of both East and West have seen Mary as the one who "shows the way" to Jesus. She is herself a sign of the Way, not *the* Way, for the Way is Jesus the Lord. Mary said "yes" to God's invitation to be the

Mother of his only Son, Jesus, true God and true man. Mary carried him in her womb and heart. We must carry him in our own daily life. Her example of fidelity to God's will and her love for Jesus motivate us to seek her intercession as we strive to become more like Jesus.

Mary is "Mother of God," not of the divine nature, but of Jesus, who is both God and man. Elizabeth proclaimed: "And why has this happened to me, that the mother of my Lord comes to me?" (Lk 1:43).

> Because of Mary's singular cooperation with the action of the Holy Spirit, the Church loves to pray in communion with the Virgin Mary, to magnify with her the great things the Lord has done for her, and to entrust supplications and praises to her (no. 2682).

Why then would prayer ever be an "agony"? Prayer can sometimes be painful because it can be a battle against distractions, fatigue, discouragement, disappointment. Those who have had "dry seasons," times when God seemed to be on an extended leave of absence, know how painful it is to continue to pray. In those times, prayer is accomplished only with difficulty through an act of the will, without emotional or spiritual consolation. The only "consolation" is the intellectual awareness that we are doing what we are supposed to do: worship God with our whole mind, soul and strength (cf. Mt 22:37).

Reflection:

- Have you ever felt lost and confused like the man in our story? How did you cope?

- Sit quietly for a while and repeat slowly and prayerfully the name of Jesus. How does this prayer affect you?

CHAPTER 6

The Battle of Prayer

"But my whole life is a prayer," objected the young woman whose mother was encouraging her to pray. "Every morning, I give my whole day to God. I use the prayer to the Sacred Heart."

Her mother argued, "But that takes just a moment while you're brushing your teeth! Don't you want to spend some time with God, getting to know him better and learning to love him more?"

"Oh, Mother!" the girl complained. "I have so little time and besides, prayer is a drag. When I go to church on Sunday it's so hard to pay attention. Boring, boring, boring! Always the same old thing! I can't keep my mind on what I'm saying."

The young woman could be anyone of any age. It is hard to pray. In fact, the *Catechism of the Catholic Church* calls prayer a battle, a battle against oneself when one feels too tired, busy or bored to pray. It is a battle against the devil who will do anything to turn us away from prayer. Moreover, to pray well presupposes an effort to live well, to live the faith, to practice virtue, to fight temptation. If a person is not living the Gospel he or she will not be able to pray. "We pray as we live, because we live as we pray" (no. 2725).

37

WE PRAY

Christians can easily become distracted by the world's mentality. Sometimes prayer seems to be only an emotional or psychological experience. It might be regarded as an escape from the real world, as a means of avoiding becoming involved in solving the problems of the world. In fact, "Christian prayer is neither an escape from reality nor a divorce from life" (no. 2727).

Sometimes, when people struggle in their effort to pray, they become discouraged and stop making the effort. Sometimes in prayer, we feel unworthy to pray because our selfishness becomes more evident and our sins are seen in their true light. Sometimes we are disappointed because God does not answer prayers in the way we think he should! Also, our own pride can get in the way—"wounded pride, stiffened by the indignity that is ours as sinners." And we resist the "idea that prayer is a free and unmerited gift..." (no. 2728).

Yes, prayer is a gift because we cannot pray without the power and prompting of the Holy Spirit (cf. Rom 8:26-27). Indeed, we cannot even say, "Jesus is Lord," except through the Holy Spirit (1 Cor 12:3).

Thinking of prayer as a gift will help us be properly disposed to pray. Prayer is a gift from God to help us become one with God. Humility is the foundation for prayer. The humble heart will not try to battle distractions, but will simply turn again toward the source and end of all prayer—our loving God. As already mentioned one popular priest-preacher has said that instead of running away from distractions, he incorporates them into his prayer: Why am I thinking of this at this time? What is God telling me about this distraction? Is this distraction rooted in one of my weaknesses, in pride, in sloth? In such a manner, one may address the problem of distraction.

The Battle of Prayer

The *Catechism* affirms this priest's view (cf. nos. 2729-2731). It states that in distraction, "all that is necessary is to turn back to our heart: for a distraction reveals to us what we are attached to, and this humble awareness before the Lord should awaken our preferential love for him and lead us resolutely to offer him our heart to be purified. Therein lies the battle, the choice of which master to serve."

The *Catechism* also speaks of dryness of soul, those times when the disciple is completely without spiritual comfort. It is a "moment of sheer faith clinging faithfully to Jesus in his agony and in his tomb."

The most common temptation is "our lack of faith," the *Catechism* tells us (no. 2732). In the midst of prayer we are besieged with thoughts of work left undone, friends we want to be with, of "a thousand labors or cares thought to be urgent" and these "vie for priority." It is a "moment of truth for the heart: what is its real love?"

Another distraction can be a sort of spiritual depression that comes from "carelessness of heart" and decreased spiritual vigilance. This discouragement is the opposite of presumption. A truly humble person will turn more eagerly to the Lord when spiritual depression is recognized for what it is: a lax spirit.

A Christian can become discouraged in prayer because God does not seem to hear. The disciple cannot "see" how God is answering the prayer. Since God does not hear, then the disciple stops praying. However, the Lord reminds us that "we do not know how to pray as we ought" (Rom 8:26). God hears and answers every prayer. God knows what is best for us. He knows the future. While something we want may seem good to us now, God, who knows the future, may well deny us our wish because of what it may mean to us later on.

Besides, the prayer of the faithful disciple is focused on God who gives, and not on *what* God gives. As the *Catechism* teaches, Christ prays for us (no. 2740). He prays in and with his disciples, so that the Father hears the prayer of Christ when we pray faithfully. "Since the heart of the Son seeks only what pleases the Father, how could the prayer of the children of adoption be centered on the gifts rather than the Giver?"

Finally, St. Paul tells us we must pray without ceasing. "Pray in the Spirit at all times in every prayer and supplication. To that end keep alert and always persevere in supplication for all the saints" (Eph 6:18).

Such perseverance and zeal can come only from love. "Against our dullness and laziness, the battle of prayer is that of humble, trusting, and persevering *love*. This love opens our hearts to three enlightening and life-giving facts of faith about prayer" (no. 2742). "It is always possible to pray.... Prayer is a vital necessity.... Prayer and the Christian life are inseparable" (nos. 2743-2745).

Reflection:

- Explain the statement: "We pray as we live and we live as we pray."

- When can distractions be considered a lack of faith?

- Name two ways in which you might overcome distractions in prayer.

CHAPTER 7

The Prayer of Jesus

The old grandmother sat alone in a room in her favorite rocking chair, clasping her rosary beads as she prayed. Her lips moved methodically, mouthing the words, "Our Father," "Hail Mary" and "Glory be."

A grandson remarked to his wife, "Poor old soul, she knows no theology, doesn't understand the Mass and can only pray her rosary."

About then, the old woman began to interrupt her formal prayers with some very informal conversation with God. "Now look, Good God. I've been asking you for four years to cure my daughter's bad shoulder. Would you please help her. It hurts her so much. And I've been praying for thirty years that Tom would stop drinking, but he's still at it. Again, please, Good God, help him get sober. And, Good God, I pray for all my children and grandchildren. Give them plenty of food, good houses and good jobs. Keep them healthy and make their marriages strong."

The grandson was deeply moved. He said, with new-found humility, "Maybe she's not so bad off after all."

Sometimes people criticize "rote prayers" as if those who use formal prayers are not really praying. It is quite possible to mumble through prayers with one's mind on the job or the Saturday fishing trip or shopping spree. But formal prayers are valuable. They help us focus on our total relationship with God and on the things that matter in prayer.

For example, the "Our Father" is truly a wonderful prayer. It puts priorities in order and even tells us what we are supposed to pray for. The next chapter will treat the Lord's Prayer in some detail. For now, we can say that since it was taught to us by Jesus, it must be perfect.

The prayer of Jesus, the "priestly prayer" at the Last Supper (cf. Jn 17), helps us focus on the mind and heart of the Father, on Jesus Christ his only Son and on the presence and power of the Holy Spirit, whom Jesus promised to send.

In that priestly prayer, Jesus acknowledges that his "hour has come" so that the Father may be glorified. He prays that we come to know the Father and himself, whom the Father has sent. Jesus reminds the Father that he has revealed his name to his disciples. Jesus affirms our faith in the truth he has preached. He prays for us in a special way, for we are his disciples, the ones who will continue the work of evangelization.

Jesus prays that we may be one as he and the Father are one. He tells the Father that he has protected his disciples and asks God to keep all of his followers in God's name.

Jesus says that he is going to the Father. He has said this publicly so his disciples can share his joy completely. Jesus knows he is about to die, but his death will accomplish the redemption of his Father's lost children. He rejoices that the Father's will would be done. He begs the Father that, as we stay behind in the world, we be protected from evil. He sends us as the Father sent him—into the world. He consecrates himself for us, that we may be consecrated in truth.

The Prayer of Jesus

Jesus prays not only for the disciples present in the upper room, but for all who would believe in him through their ministry of preaching and service. In other words, he prayed for us who believe to this day. He asks that we be brought to perfection together so that the world will know he was sent by the Father. He affirms his desire that we be with him in heaven, that we share in the inheritance of the kingdom of God.

In the final words of this prayer, spoken just before he left for the Garden of Gethsemane, knowing he would face betrayal, condemnation, torture and execution, Jesus speaks to his Father in these words: "I made your name known to them, and I will make it known, so that the love with which you have loved me may be in them, and I in them" (Jn 17:26).

John's seventeenth chapter deserves prayerful reflection. When taken in the context of the entire Last Supper discourse in John's Gospel, we can better understand the statement in the *Catechism of the Catholic Church*:

> When "his hour" came, Jesus prayed to the Father. His prayer...embraces the whole economy of creation and salvation, as well as his death and Resurrection. The prayer of the Hour of Jesus always remains his own, just as his Passover "once for all" remains ever present in the liturgy of his Church.
>
> Christian Tradition rightly calls the prayer the "priestly" prayer of Jesus. It is the prayer of our high priest, inseparable from his sacrifice, from his passing over (Passover) to the Father to whom he is wholly "consecrated."
>
> This priestly prayer of Jesus fulfills the great petitions of the Lord's Prayer, the "Our Father" (nos. 2746-2747).

WE PRAY

Reflection:

- Find a quiet place where you can be undisturbed for at least a half hour. Read prayerfully the prayer of Jesus (chapter seventeen of John's Gospel).

- What did you learn from that prayer time?

CHAPTER 8

The Lord's Prayer Revisited

The college student sat across the desk from the priest who was his mentor and spiritual director. For some time, the young man had been trying to feel closer to God. He asked the priest, "How can I understand God as my Father? I try to say the 'Our Father' but it somehow seems artificial, as if I can't mean it when I call God my Father."

The priest thought for a moment and then said, "Don't worry about it. Just keep your eyes fixed on Jesus and someday you'll discover that you really do know the Father. You'll understand how God is your Father and you will relate to him as your Father."

The priest's advice echoes Jesus' own instruction: "Philip said to him, 'Lord, show us the Father, and we will be satisfied.' Jesus said to him, 'Have I been with you all this time, Philip, and you still do not know me? Whoever has seen me has seen the Father. How can you say, 'Show us the Father'?" (Jn 14:8-9)

When the disciples asked Jesus to teach them to pray, he gave them the prayer which begins "Our Father." God is the Creator of all life. He created us from clay and breathed into us the breath of life (cf. Gen 2:4-7). Furthermore, we who were separated from the Creator through sin have been justified by the blood of Christ. In the justice of Christ, we are *privileged* to say, "Our Father."

WE PRAY

Quoting Tertullian, the *Catechism of the Catholic Church* reminds us:

> The Lord's Prayer is "truly the summary of the whole gospel." Since the Lord...after handing over the practice of prayer, said elsewhere, "Ask and you will receive," and since everyone has petitions which are peculiar to his circumstances, the regular and appropriate prayer [the Lord's Prayer] is said first, as the foundation of all desires" (no. 2761).

Our prayers reflect our relationship with God. If we only whine and beg for our needs and whims, we express a distance from God, even a certain self-centeredness and selfishness. If in our prayers we first of all praise God for his own sake, for his beauty, majesty, power, compassion, mercy and creativity, we express a better understanding both of God and of ourselves, mere creatures whose every breath depends on the goodness of the Creator.

As pointed out earlier, the Our Father is divided into two parts: praise of God, asking that his name and kingdom be made present and honored on earth, and our request for the essentials of life. In the second half of the Lord's Prayer, we place our entire lives in God's hands: our present (give us our daily bread); our past (forgive us our trespasses as we forgive others); our future (lead us not into temptation and deliver us from evil). The Our Father shows us how to ask for what we need in life, and the proper order to ask for those needs.

When people come to realize that the "Father" we turn to in the Lord's Prayer is truly "Abba" or in common usage, "Daddy," they may well experience a bit of spiritual shock and maybe even disbelief: "God, the almighty, omnipotent God, who is Trinity, who is Creator, is my 'Daddy?" Yet, that is precisely what Jesus meant. That's how close a relationship God wants with us—that we should have a trust so childlike that we come to him with open arms and trusting heart.

A father who believed in spanking was always amazed and a little ashamed that, after a spanking, his children would come to him sniffling or bawling, crawl into his lap, hug him and say, "Daddy, I love you." If only we could have that same trust and love for our Father when life deals us a few heavy blows!

The importance of this prayer is obvious when we consider that the Church prays it in the Mass, at baptisms and confirmations. As the *Catechism* states, it is prayed from an unshakable faith:

> From this unshakable faith springs forth the hope that sustains each of the seven petitions [in the Our Father], which express the groanings of this present age, this time of patience and expectation during which "it does not yet appear what we shall be." The Eucharist and the Lord's Prayer look eagerly for the Lord's return, "until he comes" (no. 2772).

If we really pray the Lord's Prayer, remembering that prayer is somehow "work," we may well develop a deeper and more trusting relationship with God.

Reflection:

- Think about your prayer and how it may have changed over time.

- If there were changes, were they for the better?

- Do you know anyone who loves and trusts God even when things go badly?

- How would you encourage a friend to trust God more?

CHAPTER 9

We Dare to Say, "Our Father"

The three-year-old boy stooped and looked under the car at his father, who was trying to install a new muffler. Suddenly the wrench slipped and Dad cracked his knuckles on the frame of the car. He groaned and moaned, scooted out from under the car and stood up, dancing from one foot to the other, holding his hurt hand.

He grew angry when his wife, who had been watching the scene from the back porch, began laughing. He asked her what was so funny. She couldn't respond because she was laughing so hard, but she pointed toward their little son. The boy was holding his hand, dancing from one foot to another, moaning and groaning—just like his dad.

Sometimes it is funny and sometimes shocking, but children do imitate their parents. In this case, we find a little child who so loved his father that he wanted to do what the father did. Jesus said quite plainly that if we want to enter the kingdom of God, we have to become like little children. Part of being childlike before God is to develop and live a deep and childlike trust, love and admiration. Maybe we could call it a strong and lively faith, not merely an intellectual assent, but we need the kind of faith that makes us want to be like our Father—holy, compassionate, kind and generous.

God is Father because he created all living creatures. From nothing, he made us and all of creation. We have a kinship with all humans, and even with stars and rocks, rivers and dew drops, eagles and slugs.

But we humans relate to God as Father in a special way, since he made us in his own image (cf. Gen 1:26-27). And we are like him, for he let us share in his creative powers: "God blessed them, and God said to them, 'Be fruitful and multiply, and fill the earth and subdue it'" (Gen 1:28a). And more, God gave humans a certain responsibility to care for the earth: "Have dominion over the fish of the sea and over the birds of the air and over every living thing that moves upon the earth" (Gen 1:28b).

Jesus Christ teaches us that God is *our* Father, not that we possess God as owners, but because he owns us. In and through Jesus Christ, we have become adopted daughters and sons, heirs of the kingdom of God. That's what faith and baptism do for us. To accept Jesus is to accept his Father, his Sonship and his inheritance. When we say "Our Father," we exclude no one.

How can we respond to such a gift? The *Catechism of the Catholic Church* says:

> The free gift of adoption requires on our part continual conversion and new life. Praying to our Father should develop in us two fundamental dispositions:

> First, *the desire to become like him....* Second, *a humble and trusting heart* that enables us "to turn and become like children": for it is to "little children" that the Father is revealed" (cf. Mt 18:3; 11:25); (nos. 2784-2785).

We Dare to Say, "Our Father"   51

Even when praying alone, the "our" in the Lord's Prayer acknowledges our mutual source of life, our mutual adoption in and through Christ and the fact that *we* are now his *people,* his *sons and daughters, heirs* with Christ to the kingdom. No believer stands alone before God.

As the *Catechism* so clearly states:

> Finally, if we pray the Our Father sincerely, we leave individualism behind, because the love that we receive frees us from it. The "our" at the beginning of the Lord's Prayer, like the "us" of the last four petitions, excludes no one. If we are to pray it truthfully, our divisions and oppositions have to be overcome (no. 2792).

If as individuals we must overcome divisions and oppositions, it stands to reason that these evils must be overcome by nations, races, classes, sexes and religions. We can begin to experience what heaven is all about in the here and now. When we pray, "Our Father, who art in heaven," we do not think of some distant unreachable paradise in which God is secluded from us. We think rather of what it means to be in God, with God, for God and of God. Quoting St. Augustine and St. Cyril of Jerusalem, the *Catechism* reminds us:

> "Our Father who art in heaven" is rightly understood to mean that God is in the hearts of the just, as in his holy temple. At the same time, it means that those who pray should desire the one they invoke to dwell in them.... "Heaven" could also be those who bear the image of the heavenly world, and in whom God dwells and tarries (no. 2794).

Oh, that delightful word—"tarries!"

WE PRAY

Reflection:

- What does it mean to you to say, "I am an heir to the kingdom of God"?

- The kingdom is in us. What does that mean to you?

- In what ways does the "Our Father" challenge people living in today's world?

CHAPTER **10**

The Seven Petitions
of the Lord's Prayer

The petitions of the Lord's Prayer are poignant, powerful and properly prioritized. We'll take a brief look at each of them, remembering that the Lord's Prayer embraces all the beatitudes because it puts God first and places us in right relationship with others.

As mentioned earlier, the Our Father is divided into two major parts. The first part places God first, where he belongs. In that first part, we address God's holiness, the need for his kingdom to come and his will be done. In the second part, we present our petitions to God. We place in God's hands our past, present and future.

Hallowed be thy name... "Holy is your name, Lord. Merely to speak your name is to speak the fullness of your majesty, your holiness, your omnipotence. To speak your name with reverence places us consciously before your throne. To speak your name irreverently is an insult to your loving kindness in revealing yourself to us. Holy is your name, Lord. May it be respected and revered by me, my neighbor and all peoples."

As the *Catechism of the Catholic Church* states, God did not lightly share his name with us (cf. no. 2810). He revealed who he was through his works to Abraham and gradually revealed it more clearly to Moses: *"I Am Who*

53

Am!" Only in Jesus Christ did he tell us he was "Father." The *Catechism* further states:

> Our Father calls us to holiness in the whole of our life, and since "he is the source of [our] life in Christ Jesus..." both his glory and our life depend on the hallowing of his name in us and by us....
>
> This petition embodies all the others. Like the six petitions that follow it, it is fulfilled by *the prayer of Christ*. Prayer to our Father is our prayer, if it is prayed *in the name* of Jesus (no. 2813, 2815).

Thy kingdom come... "Yes, Lord! Let your kingdom come! Let it come now, in my heart, in all our hearts. We know the kingdom is already here, but not yet fully. Darkness of spirit and loveless deeds hold the glory of your kingdom at bay. Please, Lord, let your kingdom come. Let love reign, and justice, and peace!"

Sometimes it is frightening to pray, "Thy kingdom come," because we actually are expressing the desire for the Second Coming of Jesus, the end of the world as we know it and the fulfillment of the kingdom of God. It is not easy to pray such a prayer when we realize how weak, sinful and unworthy we are. Only our faith in Jesus' redeeming death and resurrection enables us to jump into the Father's merciful arms and beg for his kingdom to be fulfilled here and now, in spite of our own brokenness and cowardice. As the *Catechism* says, we who pray the Lord's Prayer must realize that there is a difference between the fulfillment of God's kingdom and mere happiness on earth:

> Christians have to distinguish between the growth of the reign of God and the progress of the culture and society in which they are involved. This distinction is not a separation. Man's vocation to eternal

The Seven Petitions of the Lord's Prayer   55

life does not suppress, but actually reinforces, his duty to put into action in this world the energies and means received from the Creator to serve justice and peace (no. 2820).

Thy will be done on earth as it is in heaven... "Lord, how often we try to make ourselves happy by building sand castles and glass houses. Somehow, we sometimes forget that you are love, that you desire what is good for us, that our sin and not your will have brought pain and suffering into the world. Give us the courage and humility, dear and good Father, to pray with all sincerity and deep desire: Your will be done, here and now!"

The Father's will has been "perfectly fulfilled once for all" only in Jesus (no. 2824). Even in his terrible agony on the cross, Jesus consented to do the Father's will. We all know that famous prayer of Gethsemane: "Not my will but yours be done" (Lk 22:42).

The Scriptures startle us by saying that Jesus who was sinless, God as well as man, "learned obedience through what he suffered" (Heb 5:8). The *Catechism* goes on to say:

> How much more reason have we sinful creatures to learn obedience—we who in him have become children of adoption. We ask our Father to unite our will to his Son's, in order to fulfill his will, his plan of salvation for the life of the world. We are radically incapable of this, but united with Jesus and with the power of his Holy Spirit, we can surrender our will to him and decide to choose what his Son has always chosen: to do what is pleasing to the Father (no. 2825).

The *Catechism* also startles us by saying that our suffering, united with that of Jesus, has redemptive power and gives us a share in the mission of Jesus. Maybe we run away too quickly from pain and disappointment. Maybe we have too many aspirins and Band-Aids. Maybe we are too quick to lose ourselves in television to "relax" or "get away from it all."

Give us this day our daily bread... "Every cent we have, Father, comes from you. Our paycheck or welfare check, our food stamps or postage stamps—all come from you. We hold down jobs, but only with the talents, skills, intelligence and opportunities you give us. How helpless we would be without you! How foolish it is to forget that you are the sustainer of life as well as its author. But 'our daily bread' means so much more than food, shelter and clothing. It means education, nourishing friendships, the beauty of a dew drop on a rose, the glory of a sunset, the promise of a sunrise, the soothing caress of a loved one. Oh, thank you, Father, for your goodness!"

While a family sits at table, the toddler in the high chair points to a favorite food, and the parents immediately give the child what it wants. A baby smiles as it lifts it arms to grandma, and she immediately gathers up the child and hugs him with such joy. God loves each of us so much more than parents or grandparents ever could.

This petition concerns today, the present, and it implies that we leave the future to God. We ask only for today, trusting that tomorrow will take care of itself. We do not forsake the need to plan ahead and to save for a rainy day, but we put the future in God's hands as we look to our present situation.

We ask God to give *us our* daily bread. That implies that all of us are mutually dependent on God. It also implies that all of us together have a claim on what God provides. It is not *my* daily bread, but *ours.* As the *Catechism* states, we are not simply to sit back and expect God to work miracles to feed us (cf. no. 2830). Rather, Jesus wanted to remind us not to worry, to realize we can always

The Seven Petitions of the Lord's Prayer   57

depend on the Father. Hunger exists in the world today only because some of God's people have not shared what God has provided for all peoples (cf. no. 2831).

Certainly we must depend on God and remember that all good things come from him. However, we must use our intelligence, skills, strength and initiative to help provide for ourselves and others.

And forgive us our trespasses as we forgive those who tres-pass against us... "In the past, Lord Father, we have offended and have been offended. We need to be forgiven; we need your forgiveness. We need to be forgiven by the people we have hurt; we need to forgive the people who have hurt us. As we look at Jesus on the cross, we hear him ask you to forgive his enemies. He even excuses them—'they know not what they do.' Please help us to learn to forgive as Jesus forgives, for we must love as you love. It is frightening, Father, to realize that if we do not forgive others, we cannot be forgiven. Help us to understand this hard teaching and help us to accomplish it through your grace."

Forgiveness is not so much an action as it is a way of being, a way of life. God is love and love forgives. If we do not forgive others, we do not love. If we do not love, we cannot possibly be open to God's love for us and the forgiveness which comes to us only through love. Love is expressed in relationships, and sin weakens and destroys relationships. Unforgiveness is a sin. The *Catechism* has this to say:

> It is impossible to keep the Lord's commandment [to love one another as he loves us] by imitating the divine model from outside; there has to be a vital participation, coming from the depths of the heart, in the holiness and the mercy and the love of our God. Only the Spirit by whom we live can make

"ours" the same mind that was in Christ Jesus. Then the unity of forgiveness becomes possible and we find ourselves "forgiving one another, *as* God in Christ forgave" us (no. 2842).

Sometimes it is hard to forgive even family members whom we love. How much harder it is to forgive a real enemy—someone who has lied about us or hurt us physically, someone who has killed a loved one by accident or on purpose, someone who has cost us a job or a friend. Yet, if we are truly Christian, we must forgive as Jesus forgives.

Wise Christians know that to forgive has little to do with feelings. Love is not an emotion. To love someone is to want what is best for that person—and to do what is best. We may not "feel" as though we have forgiven because we may still be angry and hurt deeply. But if we make a conscious decision to forgive, we have forgiven. We need only to work on the hurt and the anger.

To overcome anger and resentment, we should offer the hurt for the good of the one who hurt us. That's what Jesus did, and even though we are sinners, we are now reconciled with God and are heirs of the kingdom! That's what love can do. If we really want to "get" our enemies, we should "get" them into the kingdom by making their lives "miserable" by forgiving them!

And lead us not into temptation... "We are so prone to error, Father. Don't let anything come our way that would lead us away from you."

But temptations do come. When we pray this petition, we are making what the *Catechism* calls a "decision of the heart" (no. 2848). We know from our earliest days in religious education that God will never let us be tempted beyond our strength. Sometimes we find this hard to believe, because temptation too often wins! Yet God does not

The Seven Petitions of the Lord's Prayer 59

lie. If we lived lives of prayer, depending totally on God, focusing our whole being on loving God and doing his will, temptation would be easier to resist. When temptation comes, God always provides a way to escape.

Concerning the battle with temptation, the *Catechism* states:

> Such a battle and such a victory become possible only through prayer. It is by his prayer that Jesus vanquishes the tempter, both at the outset of his public mission and in the ultimate struggle of his agony.... [Jesus] urges us to *vigilance* of the heart in communion with his own.... The Holy Spirit constantly seeks to awaken us to keep watch... (no. 2849).

But deliver us from evil... "Lord Father, look upon the crucified one. May the power of his blood flow over us so that the evil one, Satan, may not prevail in his attempts to steal us away from you. Father, this would be the ultimate injustice, that we, your own possessions, should be taken from you through sin."

It is popular in some circles to speak of evil in the abstract. Certainly evil deeds and conditions do exist in the world. When we see thousands of people starving in the Third World, or when we see bodies mangled by the tools of war, evil seems to be so large and ominous that is becomes impersonalized. But evil comes from Satan. It is committed by those who forget to seek God's will first and foremost, who seek their own desires and pleasures "no matter what."

In his prayer at the Last Supper, Jesus prayed that the Father protect us from the evil one. We had to stay in the world, but he wanted us to be strengthened against evil. His prayer touches each one of us personally, but...

...it is always "we" who pray, in communion with the whole Church, for the deliverance of the whole human family. The Lord's Prayer continually opens us to the range of God's economy of salvation. Our interdependence in the drama of sin and death is turned into solidarity in the Body of Christ, the "communion of saints" (no. 2850).

The *Catechism* continues:

...In this final petition, the Church brings before the Father all the distress of the world. Along with deliverance from the evils that overwhelm humanity, she implores the precious gift of peace and the grace of perseverance in expectation of Christ's return... (no. 2854).

He will come again. Then the kingdom for which we pray will at last be fulfilled and we shall see God face-to-face. We shall rejoice with all the saints in the glory of God. Already, in the doxology which we pray at Mass at the end of the Our Father, we praise God with eternal insight:

For the kingdom, the power and the glory are yours, now and forever!

And then all God's people say: *AMEN!*

Reflection:

• Slowly and deliberately recite the Lord's Prayer.

auline BOOKS & MEDIA

ALASKA
750 West 5th Ave., Anchorage, AK 99501; 907-272-8183

CALIFORNIA
3908 Sepulveda Blvd., Culver City, CA 90230; 310 397 8676
5945 Balboa Ave., San Diego, CA 92111; 619-565-9181
46 Geary Street, San Francisco, CA 94108; 415-781-5180

FLORIDA
145 S.W. 107th Ave., Miami, FL 33174; 305-559-6715

HAWAII
1143 Bishop Street, Honolulu, HI 96813; 808-521-2731

ILLINOIS
172 North Michigan Ave., Chicago, IL 60601; 312-346-4228

LOUISIANA
4403 Veterans Memorial Blvd., Metairie, LA 70006; 504-887-7631

MASSACHUSETTS
50 St. Paul's Ave., Jamaica Plain, Boston, MA 02130; 617-522-8911
Rte. 1, 885 Providence Hwy., Dedham, MA 02026; 617-326-5385

MISSOURI
9804 Watson Rd., St. Louis, MO 63126; 314-965-3512

NEW JERSEY
561 U.S. Route 1, Wick Plaza, Edison, NJ 08817; 908-572-1200

NEW YORK
150 East 52nd Street, New York, NY 10022; 212-754-1110
78 Fort Place, Staten Island, NY 10301; 718-447-5071

OHIO
2105 Ontario Street, Cleveland, OH 44115; 216-621-9427

PENNSYLVANIA
9171-A Roosevelt Blvd., Philadelphia, PA
19114; 215-676-9494

SOUTH CAROLINA
243 King Street, Charleston, SC 29401; 803-577-0175

TENNESSEE
4811 Poplar Ave., Memphis, TN 38117; 901-761-2987

TEXAS
114 Main Plaza, San Antonio, TX 78205; 210-224-8101

VIRGINIA
1025 King Street, Alexandria, VA 22314; 703-549-3806

CANADA
3022 Dufferin Street, Toronto, Ontario, Canada M6B 3T5; 416-781-9131
1155 Yonge Street, Toronto, Ontario, Canada M4T 1W2; 416-934-3440

Books by Henry Libersat

Pauline Books & Media

Way, Truth and Life

Do Whatever He Tells You

A Catholic Confession of Faith

Book One: *We Believe*

Book Two: *We Celebrate the Mystery*

Book Three: *We Live the Good Life*

Book Four: *We Pray*

Servant Publications

Miracles Do Happen
(co-author for Sister Briege McKenna)

Godparents

Rekindle Your Life in the Spirit
(co-author with Babsie Bleasdell)